Cambridge Discovery Education™

▶ **INTERACTIV**

Series editor: B

C000254092

ONLY IN AMERICA

A2⁺

Genevieve Kocienda

CAMBRIDGE
UNIVERSITY PRESS

Discovery
EDUCATION

CAMBRIDGE
UNIVERSITY PRESS

University Printing House, Cambridge CB2 8BS, United Kingdom

One Liberty Plaza, 20th Floor, New York, NY 10006, USA

477 Williamstown Road, Port Melbourne, VIC 3207, Australia

314–321, 3rd Floor, Plot 3, Splendor Forum, Jasola District Centre, New Delhi – 110025, India

79 Anson Road, #06–04/06, Singapore 079906

Cambridge University Press is part of the University of Cambridge.

It furthers the University's mission by disseminating knowledge in the pursuit of education, learning and research at the highest international levels of excellence.

www.cambridge.org
Information on this title: www.cambridge.org/9781107637009

First published 2014

20 19 18 17 16 15 14 13 12 11 10 9 8 7 6 5

Printed in Dubai by Oriental Press

A catalogue record for this publication is available from the British Library.

Library of Congress Cataloguing in Publication data
Kocienda, G.
  Only in America / Genevieve Kocienda.
    pages cm. -- (Cambridge discovery interactive readers)
  ISBN 978-1-107-63700-9 (pbk. : alk. paper)
  1. United States--Social life and customs--Juvenile literature. 2. English language--Textbooks for foreign speakers. 3. Readers (Elementary) I. Title.

E161.K64 2103
937--dc23

                    2013025118

ISBN 978-1-107-63700-9

Additional resources for this publication at www.cambridge.org

Cambridge University Press has no responsibility for the persistence or accuracy of URLs for external or third-party internet websites referred to in this publication, and does not guarantee that any content on such websites is, or will remain, accurate or appropriate.

Layout services, art direction, book design, and photo research: Q2ABillSMITH GROUP
Editorial services: Hyphen S.A.
Audio production: CityVox, New York
Video production: Q2ABillSMITH GROUP

Contents

Before You Read: Get Ready!

Americans love to do lots of different things in their free time. Some are interesting, some are fun – and some are a little crazy!

Words to Know

Look at the pictures. Then complete the definitions below with the correct words.

crash

motor

recreation

surfing

target

vehicle

1 _____: something that you drive

2 _____: the part of a car or other machine that makes it work

3 _____: a car accident

4 _____: something you try to hit in a sport

5 _____: a sport you do in the water

6 _____: things that you do for fun

Words to Know

Read the definitions. Then complete the paragraph with the correct form of the highlighted words.

invent: make something new

gadget: a small machine that does one thing

educate: teach; help someone learn a new thing

charity: a group that gives money, food, or help to those who need it

I give money to a **1** _____. I like it because it helps to **2** _____ children about science. The children meet after school and try to **3** _____ different things to make life easier. The children win prizes for the best, most useful **4** _____.

? PREDICT

What kinds of gadgets do you think you'll read about in this book?

CHAPTER 1

Sports and Recreation

AMERICANS LOVE TO INVENT NEW WAYS TO HAVE FUN. WHAT DO YOU THINK ABOUT THESE ACTIVITIES?

Do you like to surf? How about your dog?

Dog surfing is getting popular in California. There are even dog surfing competitions! Dogs get two **points** for lying on the surfboard, three points for sitting, and five points for standing on four legs.

There is also a competition for people surfing with their dogs, on the same surfboard. Others try to get lots of dogs on the same surfboard. The **world record** is 17 dogs surfing on one board!

Many people go to these competitions because they want to do something fun with their dogs and meet other people who like dogs and surfing. And many of these competitions raise money for charities. So, everybody wins!

People around the world love golf. But some Americans play golf in the middle of a city!

Golf is usually played on grass in the countryside. But one man, Brian Jerome Peterson, did not like seeing golf courses destroy[1] the countryside. In 1992, he decided to play golf in his town. He used a tennis ball instead of a golf ball and things like streetlights, trucks, telephone poles, and mailboxes as the "**holes**." He called it **urban** golf.

Today, people play urban golf in many towns and cities. Here are the rules:

1. Pick nine targets as "holes."

2. The ball must hit or go under big targets, and it must get near small targets, no more than one meter away.

3. Each time you hit the ball you get one point. A lost ball is three points.

4. The person with the fewest points wins.

[1]**destroy:** hurt something or change it in a bad way

ANALYZE
Why do you think some people like urban golf more than regular golf?

Usually, people use a fishing **pole** to fish. But some Americans use only their hands to catch catfish. This is called grabbling.

First, find warm water. Catfish lay their eggs in holes under water that is about 21° C. And they like to stay close to their eggs.

When you find a hole, put your hand in it and move your fingers. The catfish will think your fingers are food and will bite[2] them. Now grab the catfish quickly with your hands and pull it out of the water. You may need a friend to help you – a catfish can weigh 40 kilograms!

Grabbling is popular in the south of the USA. You can even watch it on TV!

....

[2]**bite:** use teeth to catch something

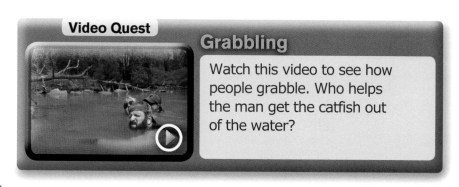

Video Quest

Grabbling

Watch this video to see how people grabble. Who helps the man get the catfish out of the water?

A fun competition for charity is the Redneck Games.

"Redneck" started as a funny name for people who work outside all the time, like farmers. They were called this because their necks get red from working in the sun.

Today, "redneck" usually describes people who don't really like things like art, museums, or

Redneck horseshoes

reading serious books. They prefer to spend time outside playing games with friends and family.

Here are some of the **events** at the Redneck Games:

Redneck Horseshoes – throwing a toilet seat onto a short pole in the ground

Watermelon Seed Spitting – spitting watermelon seeds as far as you can

Armpit Serenade – moving your hand under your arm to make sounds and "play a song"

Watermelon seed spitting

Armpit serenade

9

An ice cream cone

CHAPTER 2

Gadgets and Machines

AMERICANS HAVE INVENTED MANY USEFUL THINGS – AND SOME THINGS THAT ARE JUST FUN!

Most people like ice cream. But what happens in hot weather? You have to lick around the sides again and again because the ice cream drips[3] down the cone. Well, not anymore! The **motorized** ice cream cone turns around and around and makes it easier for you to enjoy every little bit of ice cream!

How about pasta? It's difficult to eat long pieces of pasta, right? You have to turn the pasta around your fork again and again. So try the motorized pasta fork. You put this special fork in your plate of pasta. The fork turns around and around and picks up the pasta. It does all the work for you!

[3] **drip:** fall down the side of something

A bird on its buggy

Do you want to fly like a bird? Many people do. But maybe your pet bird doesn't want to fly anymore. Maybe it wants to drive!

The motorized bird buggy is a little car for your bird. The bird "drives" the buggy with its beak. It just hits the joystick to move the buggy in any direction.

And don't worry about your bird. It's safe. If the buggy goes on small rocks or somewhere that's dangerous or difficult, the buggy stops. So, your favorite pet bird can't run into something and get hurt. Of course, it could just fly away.

Video Quest

Machines

Watch this video to learn about a special machine. What does it do for you?

Many Americans like to watch birds, even if the birds are not driving a buggy. Most bird watchers use binoculars to see birds that are far away. But some birdwatchers want the birds to come very close, so they don't have to use binoculars.

binoculars

For those people, there is a special hat that has bird feeders on it. Just put food in the feeders, put the hat on, sit quietly, and wait for the birds to come!

Many Americans also love to watch their pet fish swim around a fish tank. Now they can watch fish while they take a bath. The Fish Bath is a transparent[4] bathtub. Fish swim around the sides, and you take your bath in the middle!

....
[4]**transparent:** something you can see through, like a window

Would you like your hat to be a bird feeder, too?

Think about this: You drive to work on a sunny day with the car window open. When you get out of the car, one of your arms is a different color from the other arm. Why?

Most people put their arm up when the car window is open. So that arm, and only that arm, gets a lot of sun. One arm is your normal skin color, the other is brown – or red – from the sun. But with the Arm Mitten, that doesn't happen! Just put the Arm Mitten on the arm that is in the sun, and your arms will always be the same color.

Or maybe you're at the beach and you want a nice tan[5] on your legs. Use the Foot Elevator. This gadget helps you hold your legs up and out straight so you can get the same beautiful tan all over!

···

[5]**tan:** brown color

?

ANALYZE

Which one of the gadgets do you think is the most popular? Explain.

A soap box derby

CHAPTER 3

Crazy Vehicles

THE UNITED STATES IS A BIG COUNTRY, AND VEHICLES ARE A BIG PART OF AMERICAN LIFE. SOMETIMES, THEY'RE JUST FOR FUN.

Even children in America love cars. Some of them make their own cars and have a race called a soap box derby.

It started in 1933. Myron Scott, a photographer for a newspaper in Ohio, saw three boys racing hand-made, **motorless** cars down a hill. He wanted to have a bigger race for the boys so that he could write about it for the newspaper.

With $200 from the newspaper, he held a big race on August 19, 1933. There were 362 children in the race. They brought cars made of wooden boxes. The wheels were from baby carriages and roller skates. About 40,000 people went to see these "cars" race.

Since then, hundreds of boys and girls between the ages of 7 and 17 have raced in the largest and most famous soap box derby. It's called the All-American Soap Box Derby and takes place in Ohio every July.

The race is about winning, but it is also about education. All the children in the race are called winners. Why? Because they learned how to build their own cars. Many charities give money to the race because the race educates children about science, math, and how to enjoy a competition and have fun.

The first soap box cars used wheels from baby carriages and roller skates.

There is another kind of derby for cars in America. But it's not about racing – it's about **wrecking**!

In the late 1950s an American named Larry Mendelsohn saw that people at car races were very excited to see crashes. He thought that people would like to see a race that was *only* about crashes. He called it a demolition derby.

In a demolition derby, the cars don't try to be the fastest. They try to crash into each other. The last car that is still going is the winner. For the drivers' safety, the cars don't have glass in the windows, and the gas tank is in the back seat, not in the front of the car.

The first demolition derby was in 1958. People loved it. They are still popular today. About 1.8 billion people have watched demolition derbies in the last 25 years. And 200,000 cars have been wrecked!

In the USA, there are special neighborhoods where only people aged 55 and older can live. Some have their own swimming pools, golf courses, stores, and movie theaters. Many older people can't walk or drive cars very well, so they get around with golf carts!

Some golf carts are "tricked out" with special things that are not on a regular golf cart, like motorized fans[6] and colorful holiday lights. Some people pay $20,000 to make their carts go faster (up to 64 kilometers per hour) and to make them look like real cars.

But that's not enough for some people. They want to feel at home when they travel. These people drive art cars.

An art car is a couch with a motor in it. But it's not just a couch. People put lamps, coffee tables, or plants in them so they feel like they're driving in their living room.

Only in America!

....
[6]**fan:** a small machine that moves air around to help someone feel less hot

A special golf cart

An art car

A catapult is often used for punkin chunkin.

CHAPTER 4

Ready, Set, Go!

AMERICANS LOVE TO COMPETE, SOMETIMES IN STRANGE AND FUNNY WAYS.

In 1986, four friends wanted to know which one of them could throw a pumpkin the farthest. They decided to use a catapult. The winning pumpkin flew 38 meters!

Throwing pumpkins ("punkin chunkin") quickly became a popular competition. In 2012, in Delaware, more than 20,000 people watched 72 teams **compete** in this competition. This time, the winning pumpkin flew over 900 meters! The competition is not just fun. It also **raises** money for charities.

Video Quest

Punkin Chunkin

Watch this video to learn about this fun competition. How do people win?

Another unusual competition is frog jumping. The Calaveras County Fair[7] and Jumping Frog Jubilee is one of the oldest competitions in the state of California. It started in 1893, after the famous American writer Mark Twain wrote a funny story about a frog jumping competition.

A picture from 1893 of Mark Twain on his famous jumping frog.

Now, people from all over the world come to Calaveras County. During this four-day competition, they take care of their frogs very well. The frogs stay in the "Frog Pond." It is like a special hotel just for frogs.

People compete to see whose frog can jump the farthest. The world record holder is a frog named Rosie. In 1986 she jumped almost 7 meters!

But Americans like jumping dogs even more than they like jumping frogs.

[7]**county fair:** a fun outdoor event with food, music, dancing, and games

This dog has to jump high to catch the Frisbee.

In the 1970s, flying discs, or Frisbees™, became very popular. People enjoyed throwing them to each other at the park or the beach. But then, people started to throw them to their dogs.

In 1974, at a professional[8] baseball game between the Los Angeles Dodgers and the Cincinnati Reds, Alex Stein, a 19-year-old student from Ohio, ran out onto the field with his dog. He threw the flying disc for his dog. The dog caught it. Everyone was amazed. The baseball game stopped for eight minutes because people wanted to watch. The dog, named Ashley Whippet, ran 56 kilometers per hour and jumped 2.7 meters high to catch the flying disc!

Soon after, Stein and two other men started a Frisbee competition for people and their dogs. Then in 2000, Skyhoundz arrived.

[8] **professional:** sport played for money

Skyhoundz is the largest disc dog competition in the world. Teams of one person and one dog from all over the world compete in different regions.[9] Then all the winners from the different regions, about 200 teams, compete to see which dog can run and catch the best. And these competitions raise money for animal charities. It's a win for everyone!

People who like the water enjoy the Milk Carton Derby in the state of Washington. Every July almost 100 colorful milk carton boats of all shapes and sizes compete for $10,000 in prizes. Each boat is made of at least fifty 2-liter milk cartons. The boats must go across 366 meters of water. There are several different prizes, including one for the best-looking boat.

[9]**region:** one part of a state, country, or the world

?

EVALUATE

Why do you think many of the unusual competitions raise money for charities?

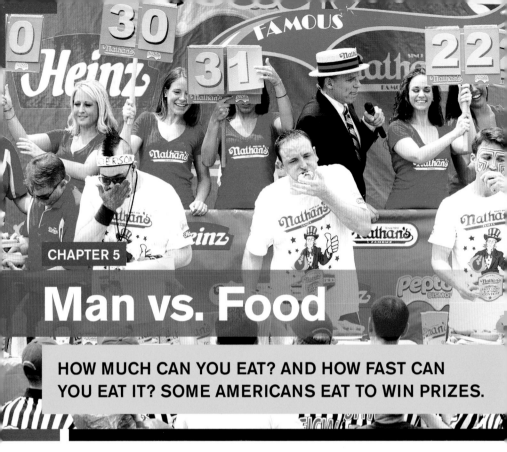

CHAPTER 5

Man vs. Food

HOW MUCH CAN YOU EAT? AND HOW FAST CAN YOU EAT IT? SOME AMERICANS EAT TO WIN PRIZES.

Nathan's Famous is a popular hot dog restaurant near the beach in New York City. On July 4, 1916, Nathan's had the world's first hot dog eating contest.[10]

The restaurant decided to have the same contest every year. In the 1990s, Nathan's hot dog eating competition became more popular. Thousands of people came to watch.

Today, there are 80–100 food eating competitions in America a year. And people don't just compete to eat hot dogs. There are eating contests with chicken, pasta, ice cream, cake, pie, and many other foods. The biggest competitions are even on TV!

[10]**contest:** a competition

So how much do the winners of these competitions eat? Here are some world records:

- Richard LeFevre: 7.5 extra large pizza slices in 15 minutes (another time, he ate 2.2 kilograms of birthday cake in 11 minutes, 26 seconds)
- Patrick Bertoletti: 4.15 kilograms of pie in eight minutes
- Don Lerman: 794 grams of butter in five minutes
- Sonya Thomas: 31.5 cheese quesadillas[11] in five minutes
- Bob Shoudt: 36 peanut butter and banana sandwiches in ten minutes

And how about hot dogs? Joey Chestnut set the world record in 2013. He ate 69 Nathan's Famous hot dogs and buns in only ten minutes!

[11]**quesadilla:** a kind of Mexican cheese sandwich

A pie eating contest

CHAPTER 6

What Do You Think?

PEOPLE IN MOST COUNTRIES DO STRANGE THINGS FOR FUN. WHAT ABOUT YOUR COUNTRY?

In 1990, a small village in Germany had the first World Beard and Moustache Championship. Men try to have the longest or most interesting facial hair. There are some really crazy styles!

And in Finland, some people think wife-carrying is a fun sport. Men carry their wives for about 250 meters, sometimes with two jumps and across some water. If a man drops[12] his wife, he can lose the race – and his wife probably won't be too happy, either.

[12]**drop:** let something or someone fall

People around the world enjoy extreme[13] ironing. Yes, ironing. It started in the UK. How does it work? You take some clothes to a dangerous outdoor place, like high up a mountain or in a fast-moving river, and, well, you iron them. In Japan, some people skateboard quickly down a hill while ironing!

Think of some unusual kinds of recreation people enjoy in your country and answer these questions:

- Who does them?
- What do people like about them?
- Do you like doing them or do you prefer watching them?
- Are there any unusual sports that are played only in your country?

What did you read about in this book that you would like to try? Why do you want to do it?

[13] **extreme:** very exciting and/or dangerous

Extreme ironing in the sky

After You Read

Read the questions and choose Ⓐ, Ⓑ, or Ⓒ.

1 Where do you play urban golf?
- Ⓐ in a place with a lot of trees
- Ⓑ in the middle of a city
- Ⓒ from a truck

2 What do you throw in Redneck Horseshoes?
- Ⓐ a toilet seat
- Ⓑ a flying disc
- Ⓒ a watermelon seed

3 Which gadget do you use inside?
- Ⓐ the birdfeeder hat
- Ⓑ the foot elevator
- Ⓒ the fish bath

4 Which vehicle can you drive to go shopping?
- Ⓐ a bird buggy
- Ⓑ a golf cart
- Ⓒ a soapbox car

5 When was the first demolition derby?
- Ⓐ 1958
- Ⓑ 1934
- Ⓒ 1865

6 What do they eat in the Nathan's Famous eating competition?
- Ⓐ pizza
- Ⓑ pies
- Ⓒ hot dogs

Complete the Sentences

Use the words in the box to complete the sentences.

charity	gadget	invent	recreation	target	world record

1 It is good to give time or money to a _____ if you can.

2 I just bought a new _____ that makes it easier to wash dishes.

3 Our town park is used by many people for _____.

4 I want to _____ something that helps people find a lost dog.

5 A golfer set the _____ for hitting a golf ball the farthest.

6 The _____ is too small and far away – I can't hit it.

Complete the Text

Use the words in the box to complete the email message.

derby	motor	vehicles	wrecks

Hi, Aunt Jane.

My friends and I are going to compete in a special

1 _____ next month. Every weekend, we work on

our **2** _____ in my family's garage. We can't have

a **3** _____, so the shape of our cars and the kind of

wheels we use are very important. I hope one of us wins and there

aren't any **4** _____!

Wish us luck!

Dan

Your Opinion

What gadget is the most useful? Which competition sounds like the most fun? Which competition would you like to compete in?

Answer Key

Words to Know, page 4
1 vehicle **2** motor **3** crash **4** target **5** surfing
6 recreation

Words to Know, page 5
1 charity **2** educate **3** invent **4** gadgets

Predict, page 5   *Answers will vary.*

Analyze, page 7   *Answers will vary.*

Video Quest, page 8
The women help him catch the catfish.

Video Quest, page 11
It helps you get up and get ready for work in the morning.

Analyze, page 13   *Answers will vary.*

Video Quest, page 19
They use a machine like a catapult to throw a pumpkin the farthest.

Evaluate, page 21   *Answers will vary.*

Choose the Correct Answers, page 26
1 B **2** A **3** C **4** B **5** A **6** C

Complete the Sentences, page 27
1 charity **2** gadget **3** recreation **4** invent
5 world record **6** target

Complete the Text, page 27
1 derby **2** vehicles **3** motor **4** wrecks

Your Opinion, page 27   *Answers will vary.*